10 Things
An Organization does
to block Customers

and

How to remove the
blocks
to unblock Customers

by
Yaqub Ali

Perfect Guidance Services for
Perfect Living

10 Things an Organization does to block Customers

Perfect Guidance Services for Perfect Living
www.pgspl.in

10 Things an Organization does to block Customers and How to
remove the blocks to unblock Customers
First publication made in Mumbai
First Edition published in 2020

Perfect Guidance Services for Perfect Living
6, E2 Batul Manzil, Burhani Centenary Park, Bustan, Surat – 395023.

Acknowledgments

Special Thanks to the team of Perfect Guidance Services for Perfect Living. The advertisers, sponsors and website visitors of Perfect Guidance Services for Perfect Living,
Also a very warm appreciation to my wonderful family who persuaded me to publish my own

writings, especially Shamoil, who forced me to start writing this book.

Table of Contents

By Yaqub Ali

Preface

Every organization needs customers. The organization by virtue of its products and services attracts customers. The marketing, promotion and publicity keeps the customers engaged. The fulfillment of an existing need or a created need of the customer leads to sale.

The organization may be a startup that has just started its operations or it can be an established organization, it is vital to avoid things that would block out customers.

These blocked out customers would keep searching for fulfilling their need and eventually land up increasing the sales of the competitor.

This book is intended to highlight 10 things that the organization does or does not do that leads to blocking customers.

Continue reading to find out if your organization is involved in any of these activities.

Chapter 1

Not defining the process clearly.

Let us start with an example. A customer wants a product or a service and the organization is offering it. The customer has the knowledge that it would fulfill his / her needs. But the customer is not able to get what the organization is offering easily. There can be many reasons why this situation can arise. But the basic cause of this issue is not defining the process clearly. The whole process from the manufacturing of the product or provision of the service to the delivery of the same is not clearly defined. Due to this it is not easily available at the stores or convenient location where the product is marketed by the organization. And it may be available where the marketing may not be done. In either ways the process of getting it becomes confusing. The customer has to find a way as to procure the product or service on their own. Such a situation may have drastic consequences on sales.

Remove the block

Create a clear process from manufacture to delivery for a product or from provision to delivery for a service. In the advertising, marketing and publicity mention how to get it or a place where customer can find out more information about getting it. If the information cannot be included in the advertisement, promotion or publicity material then give a hint or link to a place or website where the customer can get the information.

When a customer sees the advertisement, promotion or publicity material, allow details about how to procure it easily. Only when the customer is able to figure out on how to get the product or service, will the organization get the sale.

By Yaqub Ali

Unblocking Customer

When the process is defined clearly not only will the customer can easily procure the product or service but the organization will also benefit from the word of mouth that the customer will pass on regarding ease of procurement. The customer along with the use of the product will also endorse the easy procurement procedure. This word of mouth that is spread by the customer will definitely impact how others get information about what the organization offers. They too can follow the same procedure and get those products or services. So one should be very careful when defining the process of how a product or service is manufactured or provisioned till how it is delivered to the customer.

Chapter 2

Repeating procedures in Process

It is possible that there might be some pressure on defining the process in an effort to ensure that everything is completed in time. Enough time may not be available to evaluate and streamline the process. The organization may find itself in a position where some or many procedures are repeated in a process. Repetition causes the process to become less efficient. Consistency is also lost due to such duplication. Such repetitions are sometimes deliberately ignored to show more depth and engagement in the process. This also tends to make the process more complicated and difficult to understand. It is often seen that the customer is able to identify such repetition in the process in most cases. This may prove to be counterproductive for sales.

Remove the block

Time should be given to define each part of the process. Planning should be done in a proper manner when incorporating each part of the process. Important aspects can be jotted down so that the same can be given prominence in the definition of the process. If the process starts to become more complicated, then it would be wise to break it down into simplified parts. Simplification should be at both levels, at the process level and also when defining the process. A method should be used to explain this simple and easy process for the product or service to the customer. If the process is easy and simple then the customer is more likely to purchase, instead of giving up seeing the complications in the process.

Unblock Customer

The customers will see a simple and easy process and they will also spread the word about it. This creates a positive environment around the organization and what it has to offer. There are many case studies where the customers have changed their mind and purchased a product or service just because of getting information about the ease and simplicity of the purchase. This publicity is natural and will come from the customer and the organization does not have to do anything for this to happen. Such publicity can prove to be a boon for the sales and would increase the revenue of the organization. So it would be ideal to create a simple and easy process without any repetition of procedures to support increase in sales.

Chapter 3

Overlooking marketing

An organization overlooks marketing. As a result the people are not aware of what kind of products or services the organization is offering. Marketing is a channel by which the organization can inform the customer about what it has to offer. Overlooking Marketing would result in no sales happening or very less sales because of the simple reason that people are not aware of it. Using only selling methods without marketing creates demand very slowly as people due to lack of awareness will not be able to know that the product or services exist and what kind of needs can be fulfilled by using it. Without marketing most of the products will remain on the shelf of the outlets and the services will remain with the service provider. It is marketing that pushes the product or service into the hands of the customer by showing them which of their needs are fulfilled by it. It also helps to create a demand in the event that the benefits are unique in nature as compared to others already existing in the market.

Remove the block

Create unique marketing strategy for each product or service. Each product or service is unique. Even if they may seem similar there has to something different in each and every product or service. Marketing is the first introduction that the customer will see or hear about when he or she searches for options to fulfill a need. Marketing is also seen to create a need that can be fulfilled by the use of the said product or service. The marketing should be up to the point and innovative, so that it creates a good image of the organization in the minds of the customers. A good marketing strategy impacts the minds of the customers and leaves a long lasting mark. One should also make sure that, what is delivered to the customer matches with what is mentioned in the marketing materials. When the customer feels that the product or service has delivered what it had promised then that customer will continue to purchase it again.

Unblock Customer

The marketing of the product or service should contain the single pitch that highlights it and makes the product or service different from the others. This unique pitch should be communicated in a proper manner to the people who see or participate in the marketing activity. Marketing directly impacts the sale. It is good marketing that makes the customer aware of what is offered by the organization. The engagement of the customer that is created by marketing is what leads to increase in sales. Mention the need of the customer that is fulfilled very clearly in the marketing material. Seeing the fulfillment of the targeted need will entice more customers to relate to the product or service making them to buy it and use it. This is not only a repetitive process but also a viral process, because the more the customers use and like the product the more he / she will tell others about it. This will make others also to purchase and use the same. This whole process will keep repeating and the cash counter will keep ringing.

Chapter 4

Ignoring Employee Relationships

One may not believe but the relationship between the employees of the organization also has an important role to play in the sale of product or services. A negative vibe in the interpersonal relationships of the employees can create a non-conductive environment for sales to happen. The customers will not like to interact with an organization where the employees do not have good relationship with each other. A weak and unhealthy relationship between the employees of an organization brings less or no customers for the organization. Just as positive mentality attracts enthusiasm negativity repeals the confidence that the customer should have in the organization. Even the customers that purchase the products or services will stop doing so after they find out about or experience the bad relationships between employees of organization. The organization should not ignore the fact employee relationships matter and have an impact on sales.

Remove the block

Running welfare programs for employees can be a beginning. Positive interactions and training can supplement the welfare programs. When the organization regularly organizes interactive activity for the employees then they will be in a position to develop and maintain cordial relationships between their employees. This can happen easily because of the renewed understanding and bonding that is created between the employees. If the organization will kindle the positive vibes between employees, the customers will get a whiff of it and it may affect the sale of the product or service in a favorable manner. Happy employees will bring in an upswing in the graphs of sales.

By Yaqub Ali

Unblock Customers

It is mostly advertising, promotion and publicity that bring in the customers for an organization but it is also very important to maintain a pleasant atmosphere between the employees of an organization. The employees can become the best passive salesmen / saleswomen of the organization. The positive vibes between the employees of the organization can lead to more confidence and reliability on the products or services of the organization. The employees of the organization also helps the customers see more value for what the organization offers. An organization should take advantage of this opportunity. It is as simple as have a little more interaction among the employees to get a higher increase in sales. It is said that happiness attracts happiness. A bunch of happy people will raise the eyebrows of people watching from outside, because everybody wants to be happy. And in order to share and participate in the happiness, the people watching will buy the products or services.

By Yaqub Ali

Chapter 5
Losing Control over Marketing

Some organizations think that making flashy marketing materials will make customers like the product or service. For them getting attention is the only thing that they concentrate on. They bring in famous models, engage expensive advertising agencies, and spread their marketing message far and wide using multichannel communication thinking that this will make more customers to buy it. However this is not the right strategy, because marketing is the creation of an image of the organization that is portrayed on the minds of the customers. If the marketing strategy is not planned in a proper manner then it may not create any impact on the minds of the people. Flashy marketing can get the attention of the customer but will not result in sale. Losing control over marketing, losing the objective, losing focus can cost the organization leading to decrease in sales or no sales at all. This is a fairly common pitfall and organizations should maintain a strong control over marketing.

Remove the block

Marketing, more than any other activity should reflect the image of the organization. It should be clear, easy to understand and engaging. If the marketing strategy involves a generic concept, the organization should get rid of it. Marketing should be planned very strategically such that it creates an impact and appeal for the products or services. The organization should include testimonials from customers. It can also include any awards it has received for its offerings or for the process of creation of those offerings. It would also be effective to let the employees of the organization interact with customers for marketing. This creates openness and belonging in the minds of the customers to feel more engaged with the product or service. Marketing should say that the organization cares for their customer instead of asking the customer to buy the product or service.

Unblock Customer

When people are looking for products or services it is the marketing done by the organization has that will become the guide which will make them buy what the organization is offering. It is marketing that becomes the biggest signboard on the street or the hand that comes out to help the customer to get more information about the product or service. The organization should ensure that all the marketing activities are properly directed towards easy access to the products and services. Easy access can create a positive impact and also create a loop for other people to be a part of the same marketing strategy even without directly viewing or participating in the marketing process. This indirect addition happens through the satisfied customers of the organization. Further tweaking of the activities within the

33

organization should also not be ignored, because even that has the potential to make a positive difference in the sales of the product or service.

Chapter 6

Unclear about products or services

This is one of the most uncommon but it happens. Customers approach the organization hearing about the product or service through marketing; only to find out that the employees in the organization have no clue about it. Not all employees of an organization participate in the creation or research of the product or service. Given that each employee does only his / her share of work in a repeated manner, there may be no opportunity for the employee to learn about the product or service. Or the case might be that the employees are so busy in their work that they do not have the time to acquire more knowledge. Such unwelcoming employees with no or little idea about the products or features of services, an inability to explain about the product or service, can be an example, few can relate to. All this will lead to presenting an unclear picture before the customers.

Remove the block

Be as clear as possible about your products or services. That is to say that if the product is a television, then it should be shown as a television and employees should be trained to explain the uses and other details about the television. An employee stating confidently the use of a feature or explaining the benefits with thorough knowledge will be able to make a sale. If the organization is having a hard time training their employees, they should hire professional services to do so. The employees in the organization should be able to answer as many questions as possible about the product or service. This would show that the employees have a good experience using it and can explain the same to the customer.

By Yaqub Ali

Unblock Customer

Just because a product or service of a competitor is doing well in the market does not mean that organization should base the training offered for that product or service for their own offerings. Each product or service is unique. The organization should not revolve around the popular training process but should make custom made training processes. The training should concentrate on the features and benefits of their offerings. This will also highlight the uniqueness of the said product or services. The customers are always evolving and as they become smarter they keep asking more questions all the time. The clarity in the offerings can only be established when the marketing and other aspects are so tweaked that they convey this message in a clear and understandable manner. A great customer experience is what results in repeated sales and clarity about product or service is a must for great customer experience.

By Yaqub Ali

Chapter 7

Offering too much information

When customers want information about the products and services, they do not want to know about everything. They are only looking for information that would satisfy their need. Very often it is seen that the organization gives so much information that the whole marketing strategy becomes very sales oriented. In other words, it can be said that the organization tries so hard to sell its offerings that it forgets about the customers.

Educating the customers is good but that should be done in moderation with the perspective of the requirement of the customers. Information should be bifurcated into needs they satisfy. By trying to promote all the features of the product or service at once may make the customers think twice and may not result in a sale. The organization should not express what it wants to say, instead it should depict that the customer wants to hear or see, only then the customer will get a good experience and right information will be offered at the right time.

Remove the block

The content of information provided to the customer should be as per their needs, the information should be relevant to the marketing strategy that is put in place. If there is too much information to share, use different marketing strategy or information sharing methods. In this manner the customer will get that information which he / she is looking for, while all other information is available for the customer who is looking for that information. This would create a feeling of being cared for, in the minds of the customer and this feeling keeps the customer loyal to the organization.

By Yaqub Ali

Unblock Customer

Instead of having just one marketing strategy or information sharing method it would be ideal to have different marketing strategy or different information sharing methods. The different marketing strategy can concentrate on different benefits of the product or service or target different group of customers or cater to fulfilling different needs of the customer. Choice of information sharing platform should also be used keeping in mind the target audience, level of engagement and requirement of customer. Having more than one method gives more opportunities for providing better explanation with regard to the information that is being shared. These varied methods would target specific customers without affecting the others or creating a better understanding for others.

It is also easier to explain one aspect that can create a positive impact than to concentrate on multiple aspects and fail to create any impact at all.

By Yaqub Ali

Chapter 8

Not interacting with the Customer

The organization is not just about the product or service that it provides but it has to interact with the customer. A negative interaction with the company may make the customer hate what the organization is offering. This may result in the customer becoming reluctant to purchase from the organization again. A customer should get a good experience when interacting with the organization either directly or through different means. If the organization thinks that just marketing will create the necessary sale, then it is not true. Some more efforts have to be put in by the organization to create good interactive experience with the customer. On the other hand not interacting with the customer can also prove to be counterproductive as the competitor of the organization may use more interaction to attract the customer and the organization may lose that customer in the process. It is interaction that builds a relationship between the customer and the organization.

Remove the blocks

Creating interactions with the customer can be done by marketing in video format which can create or maintain an image for the organization. At the same time real time surveys, campaigns, giveaways etc. Even creating an event or sponsoring an event can make the organization create more interaction with the customers. In any case there should always be some kind of interaction between the organization and the customer. These interactions over a period of time develop a relationship between the customer and the organization. These small interactions with the customer go forward to become the building blocks of loyalty for the products or services offered by the organization in the mind of the customer.

By Yaqub Ali

Unblock Customers

The experience of the customer will have a great impact on how the word of mouth spreads in favor of the organization. The Organization should strive to offer good quality interactions with the customer. Every interaction with the customer in most cases result in increase in sales. Increase in sales is an important indicator of good interaction with customer. For the customer it develops a sense of belonging to the organization. The greater the efforts the organization puts in for interaction with the customers, the more time and energy the customer gives back to the organization. Interaction is not a one way process but it is a process of give and take. It should be a win-win situation for both the organization and the customer. A good quality interaction satisfies the needs of both. It is the satisfied customer that gets more customers for the organization.

By Yaqub Ali

Chapter 9
Not providing support

An organization would like their customers to reach out to them. If the customer has some queries the organization should provide few or multiple avenues for the customer to contact the organization to solve their queries. Likewise if the customer has some complaints the organization should provide some avenue for the customer to vent out that anger and also provide a solution for the same. For this they may need some kind of support facility. Providing just a number to contact or a contact form and forgetting about it may not be enough most of the times. Because if the customer is not able to find answers to the query or does not find somebody to hear their complaints, they might make it public. They might turn to social media. This will cause great harm to the reputation of the organization and the organization may have to spend a lot of money to undo such a negative effect that may be created.

Remove the block

Provide support for the customers by giving answers for their questions through support by call or support by chat. Ideally the support can be for 24 hours but even providing support for working hours would be great for maintaining customers. Just by offering different means of support creates a positive image of reassurance in the minds of the customer. The support factor can make a sale and bring in more sales. But it also can break a deal and decrease sales if it does not deliver what it promises. Creating more avenues for support, will make more customers come back to buy more products or services. It can also be used to provide solutions to irate customers, whereby dispute can be sorted out without involving a third party.

By Yaqub Ali

Unblock Customer

Maintain a consistent channel of support for the customers. There should be somebody to provide support facilities. In the event nobody is there for 24 hours then there should be a timeframe when the support team can be contacted. Even if it is a few, a consistent and effective support channel is better than an inconsistent one that offers great variety. This is because every time a customer uses support channel that is not working the more anger and resentment is developed against the organization. At the same time a proper support channel can provide an ideal avenue to let the customer vent out their feelings and problems such that solutions for the same can be provided or developed. Word of mouth by customers will make these consistent support channels more effective. Because when one customer directs another customer to a support channel, then the issue, in most cases, tends to get resolved. This also ensures that each customer gets a consistent experience whether the customer is new or old.

By Yaqub Ali

Chapter 10
Differentiate

An organization that is promoting the product or service in a similar manner as done by their competitors, by just making a few changes here and there, may result in promoting the products or services of their competitor. Because if the organization is not able to position its offerings in a unique and different manner then all the efforts that the organization may put in advertisement, promotion or publicity, it will end up promoting the products and services of the competitor. Customers will not be able to create a separate identity for the organization in their minds. Differentiation is not possible till the organization is able to recognize and highlight the unique features of their product over that of their competition. The organization should show the uniqueness in their offerings in a simple and explanatory manner that can be easily be understood by the customer. The difference is the uniqueness and the uniqueness is what will bring in the sales.

Remove the block

An organization should work hard to keep its products and services relevant and differentiated from their competition. This would give the organization loyal customers and steady sales. The differentiation chosen by the organization should work in favor of the organization. It should not be the case that differentiation chosen by the organization makes the product inferior to that of the competition. It is this differentiation that is a necessity for modern times. Not only does it get more sales but also creates a separate identity for the organization and its products and services. This is very important for sales but it also becomes very relevant when the competitor does something wrong on an industry level, then the blame is not automatically applied on the organization because it would be a separate identity in the minds of the customer.

Unblock Customer

Using clear differentiation not only helps in increase in customer base but also helps in creating effective interactions with the customers. The differentiated products or services stands out of the crowd of similar products and services. When the customer talks to others about the organization they also can identify the differentiated image of the organization. A unique offering of the organization can become a brand, a brand can become an image and an image always remains in the minds of the customers. When an existing customer will suggest to new customer with regard to making purchases of the products or services from the said organization, the old customer also passes the image of the product or service to that person, which makes it easier for the new customer to identify and purchase the same. It is this differentiation that creates loyalty, creates increase in sales, creates the brand image etc. in the favor of the organization.

Conclusion

An organization does a lot of research to come up with a product or service. This has to be made relevant for fulfilling the needs of the customer. The usefulness of the product and service should be clearly known to the customers. The 10 things provided here are guidelines for increasing the sales. Knowing them is necessary for each and every modern business whether it is a startup or an existing business. They will also make the organization stand out from their competitors. These are tactics that can be used directly. They can provide better customer experience and also generate a positive discussion about the products or services.

Remember it is a happy customer that gets more happy customers.

About Perfect Guidance Services for Perfect Living

Organizations benefit greatly from Occupational counseling. Perfect Guidance Services for Perfect Living offers the best occupational counseling services to S2B (Supplier to Business), B2B (Business to Business) and B2C (Business to Customer) organizations. The focus would be to resolve any issues or problems faced by the organization which may be causing decrease in sales or lack of sales resulting in loss or may even lead to closure in the future.

Occupational Counseling helps the organization to become more profitable. As an Occupational Counseling service provider, Perfect Guidance Services for Perfect Living has the potential to serve its customers with the ideal business tactics and strategies that can deliver positive business results.

Occupational Counselors at Perfect Guidance Services for Perfect Living have the expertise to provide counseling for organizations from different industries and having varied number of employees. All businesses can avail of occupational counseling services.

About the Author

Y. Ali is a ghostwriter who has written more than 171 books in more than 22 years, a practicing occupational counselor for more than 19 years and a philosopher who has done in depth research in many fields including medicine, space and new inventions. Many of the books authored by him have been bestsellers, some have been widely popular and few of them have been gained international acclaim.

By Yaqub Ali

Visit the website of Yaqub Ali, at www.yaqubali.com for latest information, counseling services and to join him on his social sites like Facebook, Twitter and Linkedin.

Yaqub Ali is acclaimed to be very research oriented as he does a lot of research before putting it into words. He also uses simplified language and engaging tone which keep the reader engrossed from beginning to the end. He is brilliant with words, is very appealing in the views that he expresses and writes what he believes.

Upcomming Works by the Author Yaqub Ali

20 more books in the series Occupational Counseling

5 books on Covid 19

15 short stories books

50 self help books